CW00894813

JOURNAL of
THE PLAGUE YEAR

COLD WAR STEVE

JOURNAL of
THE PLAGUE YEAR

(PAGE 3) *Trumpscape.*
4   (ABOVE) *Effluent.*

INTRODUCTION

On a bleak winter's day in 2004, I was trudging down the hard shoulder of the M42 southbound. Miles of traffic cones needed cleaning. Katy (my girlfriend – now wife) was pregnant with our first child, we had no stable accommodation, and I was hideously in debt; I was completely overwhelmed with worry and despondency. Keeping my head down so that passing motorists wouldn't see my red, teary eyes (and call the police, reporting a deranged-looking road-worker), I suddenly spotted something in the gravel and dust at the foot of the crash barrier. I leant down, picked it up and found Guru Nanak, the founder of Sikhism and first of the ten Sikh Gurus, waving at me from inside a snow globe. How had it got there? It couldn't have been thrown from a car window – it had been standing upright, and there wasn't a scratch on it. I was convinced that it had been placed there for me to find. But why? To explore the Guru's teachings? Or simply to get pleasure and comfort from its very existence? I shook it and held it aloft. I smiled.

31 January 2020 was 'Brexit Day' – Britain had left the European Union. My detractors (yes, there are some, believe it or not) were all saying the same thing: 'What you gonna do now Brexit's done? Remoaning prick!' – or words to that effect. They had a point, to be fair; it's no secret that my anxieties and general disgruntlement over Brexit had driven most of my output for the past couple of years. But those feelings hadn't gone away, and neither had the people who had orchestrated our disastrous exit. My answer to the jeering Brexiteers, therefore, was that I would continue to shine a light on the fuckers. However, with the exception of the US elections in November, 2020 was probably going to be a bit of a non-event – a slow news year. My output on Twitter would consequently be much less prolific. Right?

From mid-February and into March, as the coronavirus extended its tentacles around the globe, I wasn't certain whether I should be satirizing something that was so foreboding. Our plucky PM saw no reason to attend five Cobra meetings on this emerging pandemic, but people were scared. Really scared. People were dying. Shops had run out of toilet roll.

My wife Katy is a carer at a home for dementia patients. She was coming home from work in tears – telling me about the death of yet another resident. She explained that patients were being sent directly from hospitals into the home, without having had a test for Covid-19. As a consequence, the virus tore through the residents. At this time, Health Secretary Matt Hancock was boasting about the 'protective ring' he had placed around the care system. I couldn't hold back any longer.

I have never shied away from dark themes, but my first Covid-related collages were released very tentatively. It soon became clear that I wasn't alone in becoming increasingly horrified at the way the government were handling the country's response to the pandemic. A couple of my followers on Twitter remarked that they knew when I was really angry about something, as my production rate increased significantly. Indeed it had. I find great relief in being able to channel my rage and fears into my art. I will always be so grateful for my audience on Twitter and the communal interaction with people who were all troubled and affected by what was happening, but finding solace in a shared exasperation at the daily fuck-ups of the people in charge – and especially so at a time when so many people were being kept apart.

Social media can be a toxic, dispiriting place. My hope is that someone scrolling through all the hatred and lies suddenly lands on one of my pictures and pauses. Smiles. You're not alone. This shall pass.

Cold War Steve – Thursday 29 July 2021

PLATES

👉 **30 January 2020**

Brexit Eve. At 11.00 p.m. tomorrow, the United Kingdom, after forty-seven
years of membership, will officially leave the European Union.

🖎 **31 January 2020**

Brexit Day. Let's fucking party!

☞ 20 March 2020

Yesterday, a few days before announcing the first national lockdown, the PM stated that the UK could 'turn the tide of coronavirus in 12 weeks'. Morale was also buoyed by the news that Boris Johnson's partner, Carrie Symonds, was pregnant.

☞ 23 March 2020

Yesterday, Downing Street rejected claims that chief advisor Dominic Cummings, arguing against stricter measures to contain the virus, stated that 'if that means some pensioners die, too bad'. A first appearance here for Dr Harold Shipman, Britain's most prolific serial killer, whose victims were all vulnerable elderly people.

☞ **26 March 2020**

Reports surface that multi-millionaire chef Gordon Ramsay has sacked 500 of his workers and is paying their notice with the taxpayer-funded furlough scheme.

☞ 28 March 2020

The PM is down! Johnson has tested positive for the coronavirus.
Background painting here is *The Fall of the Damned* by Peter Paul Rubens.

☞ 5 April 2020

Renowned non-epidemiologist and *Daily Mail* columnist Sarah Vine tweeted yesterday that she supports the use of the anti-malaria drug Hydroxychloroquine for the treatment of Covid-19. In this composition, Ms Vine and then husband Michael Gove emerge from Edward Hopper's *Drug Store*.

🖝 15 April 2020

The country is suffering a woeful lack of PPE. Nurses and doctors resort to wearing bin bags for aprons.

🎺 **28 April 2020**

The President of the United States is guzzling anti-malarial medication and talking about the benefits of drinking bleach. The backdrop painting used here is *The Quack* by Jan Steen.

🐾 4 April 2020

Cummings and Johnson both have Covid-19. Background here is based on Edward Hopper's *Excursion into Philosophy.*

19

☞ 8 April 2020

Multi-billionaire Richard Branson pleads with the UK Government for a £1.2bn bailout package for his airline. Tim Martin of Wetherspoons, who had branded the national lockdown as 'over the top', advises his 40,000 employees that he will not be making any further wage payments – and suggests they go and work at Tesco instead.

☞ 8 April 2020

Hogarth's *Gin Lane*, reimagined for Johnson's Britain.

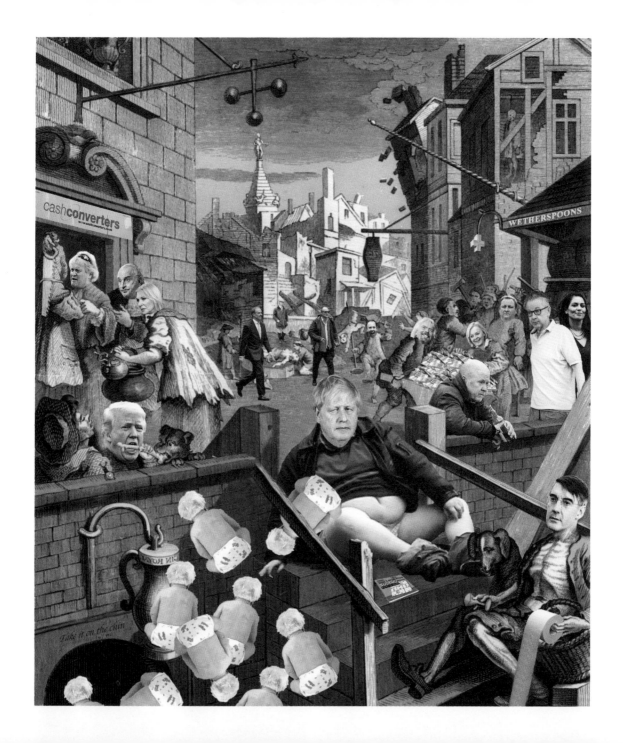

25 April 2020

As venal billionaires lay off workers and clamour for government handouts, 99-year-old Captain Tom Moore totters up and down his garden to raise money for the NHS.

☞ 10 **May** 2020

The three-part slogans are coming
thick and fast.

27

🎺 4 June 2020

Three days ago, Donald Trump ordered his own brand of Stormtroopers to forcibly remove peaceful demonstrators, protesting the killing of George Floyd, from the front of the White House, for his photo opportunity outside St John's Episcopal Church.

☞ **23 May 2020**

Yesterday, reports emerged that Dominic Cummings had breached lockdown rules, travelling over 250 miles from his London home to Durham in April.

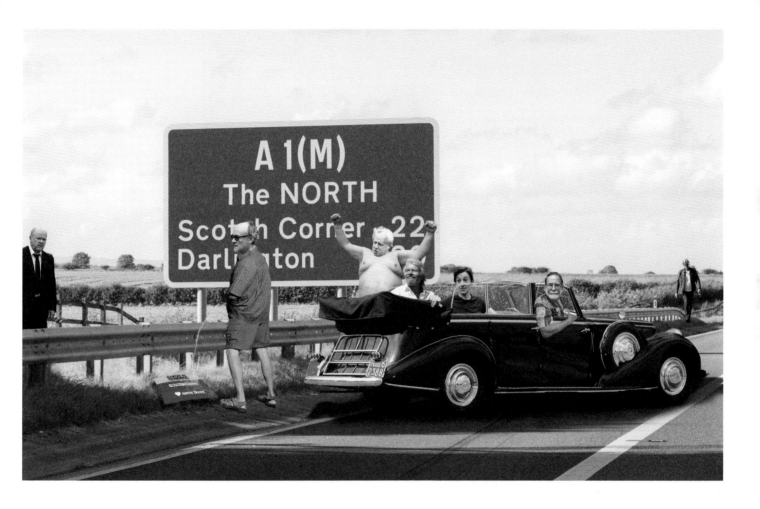

Further revelations regarding Cummings' lockdown-breaching trip to Durham surface.
The outrage of a nation of hitherto lockdown-rule-adherers, united in indignation, is palpable.

☞ 17 May 2020

(OPPOSITE) Trump's handling of the pandemic is turning out to be just as inept as that of Johnson's cabinet of talents. The background painting here is *Death Playing the Violin* by Frans Francken II.

☞ 25 May 2020

(ABOVE) Cummings is afforded a unique opportunity to explain his lockdown breach in a bizarre press conference in the Rose Garden at Downing Street. The background here is inspired by a witness who overheard Cummings remarking on the 'lovely bluebells' in a wood near Barnard Castle.

👉 **13 May 2020**

Dr Shipman surfs the impending second wave. The elderly and vulnerable are
unaware that come the autumn, Johnson would argue against a further lockdown,
as 'the people who are dying are essentially all over 80'.

The coronavirus death toll in the UK is approaching 40,000. Elderly patients are sent directly from hospitals, untested, back into care homes, in spite of Health Secretary Matt Hancock's 'protective ring'. The background here is St Lawrence's Church in the 'plague village' Eyam.

☛ 29 May 2020

Donington Park Services on the M1. Where
Dominic Cummings could have stopped –
to stretch his legs and scatter his virus –
on his way up to Durham from London.

27 May 2020

Cummings claims that a 60-mile round trip from Durham to Barnard Castle (on his wife's birthday) had merely been in order to test his eyesight.

🖙 8 June 2020

Anti-racism protestors in Bristol pull down the statue of slave trader
Edward Colston and throw it into the river.

👉 10 June 2020

Reverend Johnson presides over a perpetual funeral service.
Family and loved ones are not allowed to attend.

🐾 12 June 2020

The 'expendables' are helped on their way.

☞ 9 July 2020

'Congratulations, comrade Cummings. Your work here is almost done.'

43

☞ 15 July 2020

It is announced that from 24 July, in an effort to help prevent the spread
of the virus, supermarket shoppers will be required to wear face masks.
The professional contrarians are incensed by this despotic attack on liberty.

🐾 16 July 2020

The nerve centre of the 'world-beating' track-and-trace system.

☞ 24 July 2020

Yesterday, President Trump displayed the superiority of his mental agility
once again, revealing in an interview that he'd recently undertaken an extremely
difficult cognitive test: 'Person, woman, man, camera, TV. Nobody gets it in order;
it's actually not that easy. But for me, it was easy. And that's not an easy question.'

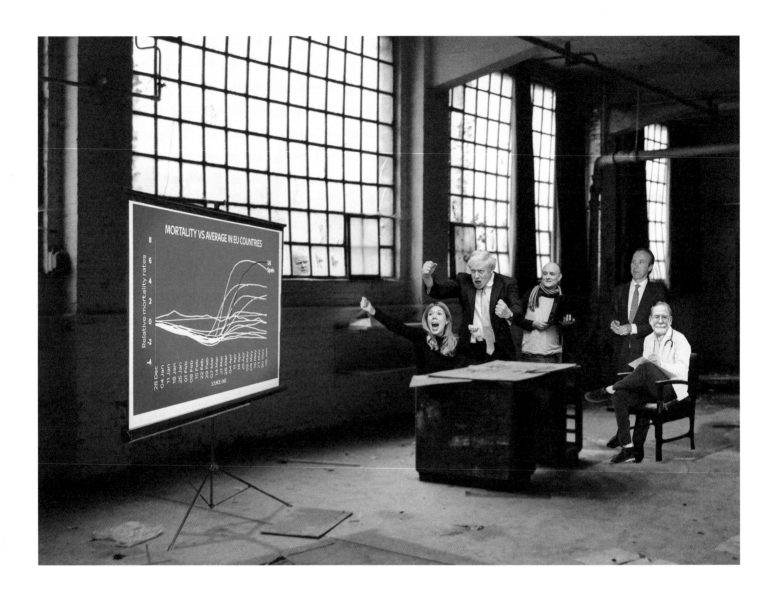

☞ 30 July 2020

Team Johnson celebrate the UK becoming the champions of Europe!

🖝 9 August 2020

'Tis the season for Nigel Farage to patrol the English Channel.

☞ 13 August 2020

Note the contrived contrarianism of Dom Cummings – he's simply too brainy and brilliant to notice that his jumper is inside out.

☞ 16 August 2020

Dreaming of what may become of this government when this is all over.

☞ 19 August 2020

The body of a sixteen-year-old
Sudanese migrant is found washed up
on a French beach. The response from
the Home Office is characteristically
devoid of any compassion.

☞ **29 August** 2020

Thousands attend an anti-mask, anti-lockdown, anti-science demonstration in London.

🖝 13 September 2020

Dominic Cummings and the Johnson cabinet are responsible for preventing
the opening of the Seventh Seal. My sense of hopelessness is overwhelming.

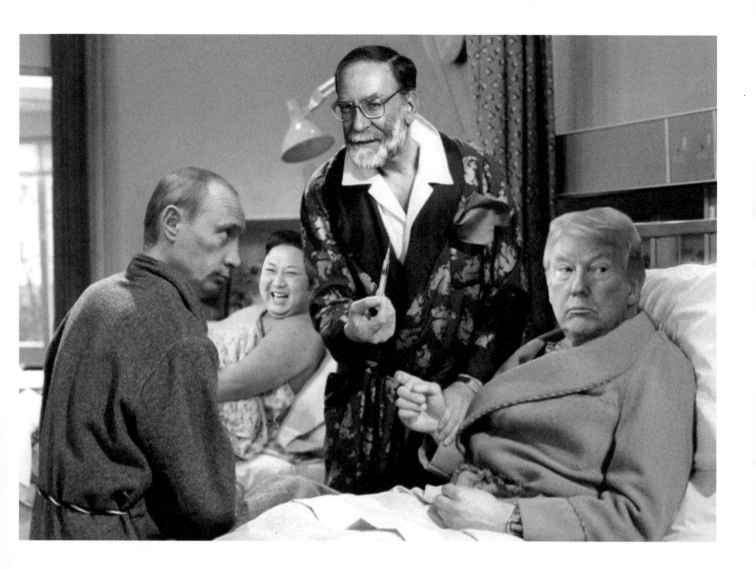

☞ 3 October 2020

Yesterday, Donald Trump tweeted that he had tested positive for Covid-19.
He would emerge from hospital a few days later, claiming that his immunity to
the virus amounted to a 'protective glow'.

BUSINESS NOT AFFECTED
FREEHOLD
FOR SALE
Anthony Green
& Spencer
071-935 2335
KWIK SAVE FOODSTORE
KWIK
SAVE
FOODSTORE
KWIK SAVE
NO NONSENSE FOODSTORES
WE SIMPLY
SAVE YOU

☞ 12 October 2020

The US election is just weeks away, and there's a growing sense that the outcome may not be the one the Brexit government had always hoped for.

7 October 2020

The 'world-beating' test-and-trace system in full swing.

⮞ 8 October 2020

The arts have been hit especially hard during the pandemic. Chancellor of the Exchequer Rishi Sunak suggests that artists and performers retrain in something like 'cyber' instead.

☞ 23 October 2020

Two days ago, Tory MPs voted against extending free school meals to disadvantaged children during the holidays. Footballer Marcus Rashford – who has been campaigning tirelessly for the meals to continue in holiday periods – tweets immediately after the result, urging MPs not to 'turn a blind eye to the needs of our most vulnerable children'.

☞ 7 November 2020

It's official – Joe Biden has won the
election! Trump refuses to accept the
result, obviously.

8 November 2020

Trump's deranged behaviour after the US election result shocks the world. We should perhaps remember who were his biggest boot-lickers from this side of the Atlantic.

🔖 28 October 2020

The government aren't backing down on their decision
not to extend free school meals during the holidays.

🏴 **12 November 2020**

The Ship of Fools 2020.

☞ 13 November 2020

Breaking news... Dominic Cummings has
been 'booted out' of Downing Street with
immediate effect!

☞ 18 November 2020

Construction begins on an enormous lorry park in Kent
to cope with the impending chaos that Brexit will bring.

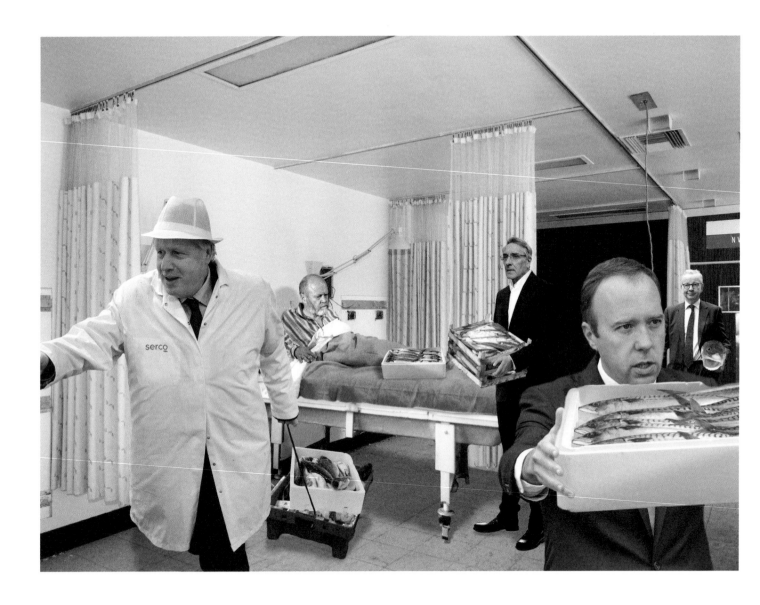

According to prominent Brexiters, such as Conservative MP John Redwood,
the only tangible benefits of Brexit are blue passports and... FISH!

✆ 10 December 2020

Our noble statesman Boris Johnson goes to Brussels to meet with European Commission
President Ursula Von der Leyen, for a 'make-or-break Brexit dinner'.

☞ 7 January 2021

Last night, Trump supporters (under his incitement) stormed the US Capitol. Britain's biggest Trump supporters suddenly go very quiet on the matter.

🖝 **18 January 2021**

It's just two days until Joe Biden moves
into the White House.   81

☞ 19 January 2021

In exactly one week's time, the UK's Covid-19 death toll will reach 100,000.

☞ 13 January 2021

(OPPOSITE) Pictures emerge of the new 'free school meals' food parcels,
which include such delights as half a bell pepper, a couple of Frubes and a potato.
The painting I've used here is *The Oyster Dinner* by Jean-François de Troy.

☞ 3 February 2021

(ABOVE) The Irish border: Johnson's Brexit deal appears anything but 'oven-ready'.

Heathrow

➳ 3 February 2021

Concerns of new coronavirus variants
entering the country are escalating.
PM Johnson dismisses calls for tougher
border restrictions as 'not practical'.

🖐 3 March 2021

Questions are raised as to who paid
for the six-figure refurbishment of
Johnson's Downing Street flat (which
included £840-a-roll gold wallpaper).

🏳 5 February 2021

The anti-maskers and covid conspiracy theorists are protesting again.

🖎 19 February 2021

The baying mob.

☞ 5 March 2021

The government rewards heroic NHS workers with a 1% pay rise (averaging an extra £3.50 a week). The background here is William Hogarth's *An Election Entertainment*.

☞ 9 March 2021

It is announced that Andrew Neil's 'anti-woke' GB News will be launched later in the summer.

☞ 11 March 2021

Neil reveals that his news channel will include a feature called 'woke watch'.

☞ 13 March 2021

A peaceful vigil for Sarah Everard, a 33-year-old woman murdered by a serving
Metropolitan police officer, is violently broken up by police.

one amazing year

🔖 23 March 2021

(OPPOSITE) It is the anniversary of the first lockdown. 126,000 deaths
have been attributed to Covid-19 in the UK.

🔖 27 March 2021

(ABOVE) Hairdressers will be allowed to open their doors again from 12 April.

🖙 **25 March 2021**

Every Tory MP suddenly seems to have a union flag in the background of their Zoom interviews.

The real state of the nation.

👉 15 March 2021

Home Secretary Priti Patel is pushing an 'anti-protest' bill through Parliament. The background here is a still from Mike Leigh's *Peterloo*.

⌖ 1 April 2021

(ABOVE) Revelations emerge of Johnson's historic affair with
Jennifer Arcuri, but are met with a distinct lack of opprobrium.

⌖ 30 March 2021

(OPPOSITE) There doesn't seem to be any mention of Johnson's affair
(or indeed any of his numerous indiscretions) in the UK media.

☞ **8 April 2021**

Rioting in Belfast enters its fifth night. The Good Friday Agreement is looking increasingly fragile.

☞ **14 April 2021**

Lobbying, corruption, cronyism, sleaze, gross incompetence...
but the Tories don't drop any points in the opinion polls.

☞ 21 April 2021

Leaked emails allege that in April last year, the PM privately assured billionaire inventor James Dyson that he would 'fix it' so that the firm's employees would not pay extra tax if they came to the UK to make Dyson ventilators.

🖙 22 April 2021

Dyson never supplied any ventilators to the NHS in the end.

🏴 **24 April 2021**

The dysfunctionality of the government surpasses anything previously seen on *The Jeremy Kyle Show*.

☞ 25 April 2021

The absolute worst, most despicable, shameless, incompetent, mendacious
Prime Minister of all time – and yet the polls indicate that Johnson's popularity
with the general public hadn't wavered. There were many times when I thought,
"what's the fucking point?"

Johnson denies that he responded 'no more fucking lockdowns –
let the bodies pile high in their thousands' when tasked with approving a
second England-wide lockdown in late 2020.

Welcom
Hartlep

Home of the N
Museum of the R

☞ 5 May 2021

The Conservatives defeat Labour in the
Hartlepool by-election.

☞ 10 **May** 2021

For fuck's sake, people - he isn't wearing anything at all!

☞ 21 May 2021

Home Secretary Priti Patel – who was pictured last week ghoulishly
watching immigration enforcement officers conducting house raids –
unveils plans for a sweeping immigration overhaul.

☞ **12 May 2021**

Private Eye Magazine reveals that a county court judgment (CCJ) for unpaid debt had been made against one Boris Johnson, address 10 Downing Street, in October last year – and six months on, it still hasn't been paid.

☞ 16 May 2021

Recognizing the signs of onset,
I attempt to avoid falling into a
debilitating Brexit/pandemic-induced
torpor by unleashing all my anxieties
and anger into one photomontage.
The original painting here is *Allegory of
Abuses by the Authorities of Church and
State*, by Gillis Mostaert.

🖐 26 May 2021

Keir Starmer, opening Prime Minister's Questions, asks: 'This morning the
Prime Minister's former closest adviser said "when the public needed us most,
the Government failed" – does the Prime Minister agree with that?' Mr Johnson replies:
'No, all those matters will be reviewed in the course of the public inquiry that I have
announced. I notice he is fixated, as ever, on the rear-view mirror.'

HANCOCK FAMILY BUTCHER

LICENSED TO DEAL IN DEATH

PORK LAMB BACON MAN

Protective Sausage Rings

ORDER THE REAL TASTE OF CHRISTMAS HERE
TRADITIONAL FRESH TURKEYS
YOU DESERVE IT

FRESH KEBAB SOLD HERE

At any time

PRACTISE SOCIAL DISTANCING
2m

🔖 **27 May 2021**

An increasingly vengeful Dominic Cummings publishes WhatsApp messages
he claims to have received from the PM in March last year, in which Johnson
describes Health Secretary Matt Hancock as 'totally fucking hopeless'.

🐾 **30 May 2021**

Three Weddings and 129,000 Funerals. Twice-divorced Alexander Boris De Pfeffel Johnson marries Carrie Symonds in a secret ceremony at the Catholic Westminster Cathedral.

☛ 26 June 2021

Health Secretary Matt Hancock, who has remained in post throughout the pandemic in spite of his lies, ineptitude and cronyism, is finally brought down after CCTV images show him in a 'steamy clinch' with his married aide Gina Coladangelo.

First published in the United Kingdom in 2021 by
Thames & Hudson Ltd, 181A High Holborn, London WC1V 7QX

Cold War Steve – Journal of The Plague Year
© 2021 Thames & Hudson Ltd, London

Illustrations and captions © 2021 Christopher Spencer
Introduction © 2021 Christopher Spencer

British Library Cataloguing-in-Publication Data
A catalogue record for this book is available from the British Library

ISBN 978-0-500-02515-4

Printed and bound in Slovenia by DZS-Grafik d.o.o.

Be the first to know about our new releases,
exclusive content and author events by visiting
thamesandhudson.com
thamesandhudsonusa.com
thamesandhudson.com.au